Omar can Help

by Lynne Rickards
illustrated by Moni Perez

CAMBRIDGE
UNIVERSITY PRESS

In association with

Institute of Education

Zara and Leila were making a house.

'This roof is no good!'
said Zara.

'Can you help us, Omar?'

Omar knew what to do.
'You need one more stick here,'
he said.

'Thank you, Omar,'
said the girls.

Beno's tower was wobbling.
It was going to fall.

'Oh, no!' said Beno.
'Can you help me, Omar?'

7

Omar knew what to do.

'Thank you, Omar,'
said Beno.

At snack time, they went
outside.
Zara had a cake to share.

'Oh, no!' said Kofi.
Omar knew what to do.

He jumped up to get
a new plate for Kofi.

Oh no! Omar fell down.
'Help!' he shouted.

Everyone said, 'We can help!'
'Thank you,' said Omar.

Omar can Help ✒ Lynne Rickards

Teaching notes written by Sue Bodman and Glen Franklin

Using this book

Developing reading comprehension

This is a story about Omar and his friends. Omar is keen to help but often his best intentions go wrong.

Grammar and sentence structure

- Simple sentence structures repeated in different contexts.

- Repetition of spoken phrases and punctuated speech to aid expression and reading for meaning.

Word meaning and spelling

- Opportunity to rehearse regular phonically decodable words ('can', 'help', 'stick').

- Vowel digraph /ew/

- Explore compound words ('everyone', 'outside')

Curriculum links

Mathematics – Zara brought a cake to share. How would she divide it up to ensure there was a piece for everyone?

Design and Technology – Omar helped the girls fix the roof of their house. Explore ways of building different roof shapes.

Learning Outcomes

Children can:

- read simple words by sounding out and blending phonemes left to right

- use syntax and context when reading for meaning

- locate, read, and write high-frequency words.

A guided reading lesson

Book Introduction

Give each child a book and read the title to them. Point out Omar on the front cover,

and his friends Zara and Leila. *We are going to meet these characters and some of Omar's other friends as you read this book.*

Orientation

Discuss why the children think the book might be called 'Omar Can Help'. Use the illustrations on the front and back covers to help to identify the things Omar does to help his friends.

Give a brief overview of the book, using the verb in the same form as it is in text.

This is a book about Omar. His friends asked him to help. He always knew what to do.

Preparation

Pages 2 and 3: *Oh dear, the roof on their house is no good. Zara says 'Can you help us, Omar?'. Find that part in the story* (children identify the speech marks punctuating Zara's speech). *Let's read it and make our voices sound like we are asking a question.*

Check that all children are using phonemes to read the phonically regular words 'can' and 'help'. Practice saying the words slowly.

Page 4: *'Omar knew what to do.'* is a refrain throughout the book. It is important to establish one-to-one finger matching and accurate reading of this sentence.

Discuss: *What did Omar know how to do? Yes, he put one more stick in to hold up the roof.*

Pages 6 and 7: *This is Beno. He is Omar's friend, too.* Ask the children to find Beno's name in the text. Discuss what is happening in the picture, and revisit the phrase *'Can you help me, Omar?'* using speech marks as previously.

Page 10: Establish that it is snack time, and that Zara has brought a cake to share: *Look, she has cut it into slices to share with her friends, but – Oh dear! Look at Beno's face.*